OUR FAVORITE FOODS

Chocolate Chip Cookies

by Joanne Mattern

BELLWETHER MEDIA • MINNEAPOLIS, MN

Note to Librarians, Teachers, and Parents:

Blastoff! Readers are carefully developed by literacy experts and combine standards-based content with developmentally appropriate text.

Level 1 provides the most support through repetition of high-frequency words, light text, predictable sentence patterns, and strong visual support.

Level 2 offers early readers a bit more challenge through varied simple sentences, increased text load, and less repetition of high-frequency words.

Level 3 advances early-fluent readers toward fluency through increased text and concept load, less reliance on visuals, longer sentences, and more literary language.

Level 4 builds reading stamina by providing more text per page, increased use of punctuation, greater variation in sentence patterns, and increasingly challenging vocabulary.

Level 5 encourages children to move from "learning to read" to "reading to learn" by providing even more text, varied writing styles, and less familiar topics.

Whichever book is right for your reader, Blastoff! Readers are the perfect books to build confidence and encourage a love of reading that will last a lifetime!

This edition first published in 2020 by Bellwether Media, Inc.

No part of this publication may be reproduced in whole or in part without written permission of the publisher. For information regarding permission, write to Bellwether Media, Inc., Attention: Permissions Department, 6012 Blue Circle Drive, Minnetonka, MN 55343.

Library of Congress Cataloging-in-Publication Data

Names: Mattern, Joanne, 1963- author.
Title: Chocolate Chip Cookies / by Joanne Mattern.
Description: Minneapolis, MN : Bellwether Media, 2020. | Series: Our favorite foods |
Includes bibliographical references and index. | Audience: Ages 5-8. | Audience: Grades 2 to 3. |
  Summary: "Relevant images match informative text in this introduction to chocolate chip cookies.
  Intended for students in kindergarten through third grade"-- Provided by publisher.
Identifiers: LCCN 2019026974 (print) | LCCN 2019026975 (ebook) |
  ISBN 9781644871430 (library binding) | ISBN 9781618918192 (ebook)
Subjects: LCSH: Chocolate chip cookies--Juvenile literature.
Classification: LCC TX772 .M295 2020 (print) | LCC TX772 (ebook) | DDC 641.86/54--dc23
LC record available at https://lccn.loc.gov/2019026974
LC ebook record available at https://lccn.loc.gov/2019026975

Text copyright © 2020 by Bellwether Media, Inc. BLASTOFF! READERS and associated logos are trademarks and/or registered trademarks of Bellwether Media, Inc.

Editor: Kate Moening   Designer: Jeffrey Kollock

Printed in the United States of America, North Mankato, MN.

Table of Contents

Fresh From the Oven	4
Chocolate Chip Cookie History	8
Chocolate Chip Cookies Today	14
Glossary	22
To Learn More	23
Index	24

Fresh From the Oven

What is that wonderful smell? Your cookies are done baking! These tasty treats will make a **delicious** snack.

Chocolate chip cookies are a favorite dessert or snack. Many people enjoy them with a glass of milk.

Chocolate chip cookies are made of sugar, flour, eggs, butter, and more. The most important **ingredient** is chocolate chips!

How to Make Chocolate Chip Cookies

1. Mix ingredients in a bowl
2. Drop dough onto a baking sheet
3. Bake in the oven
4. Enjoy chocolate chip cookies!

cookies baking in oven

Once the ingredients are mixed together, the cookies bake in an oven.

Chocolate Chip Cookie History

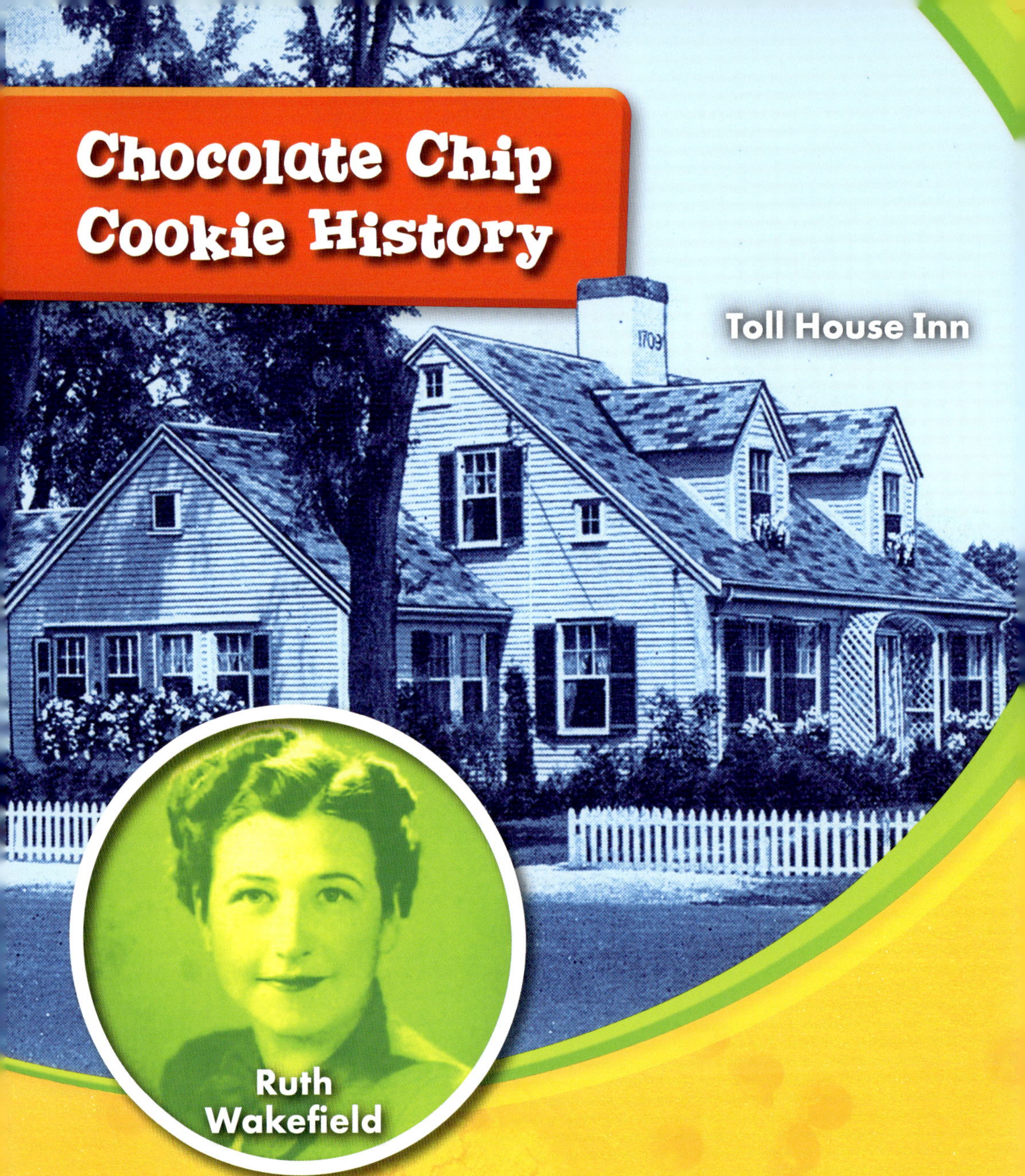

Toll House Inn

Ruth Wakefield

A baker named Ruth Wakefield invented chocolate chip cookies in the late 1930s.

She owned a restaurant in Massachusetts called the Toll House Inn. It was famous for its tasty desserts.

Easy Chocolate Chip Cookies

Ask an adult to help you with this classic recipe!

Tools

- large bowl
- mixer
- spoon
- baking sheet

Ingredients

- 1/2 cup butter (melted)
- 1/2 cup sugar
- 1/4 cup brown sugar
- 1 egg
- 2 teaspoons vanilla
- 1 3/4 cups flour
- 1/2 teaspoon baking soda
- 1/2 teaspoon salt
- 1 cup chocolate chips

Instructions

1. Preheat oven to 350 degrees Fahrenheit (177 degrees Celsius).
2. Mix melted butter, sugar, and brown sugar in a bowl.
3. Add egg and vanilla. Mix well.
4. Add flour, baking soda, and salt. Stir.
5. Add chocolate chips. Stir.
6. Scoop 1-inch balls of dough onto a baking sheet. Place about 1 inch (2.5 centimeters) apart.
7. Bake in the oven 7-10 minutes, until puffy.

Ruth served **butterscotch** cookies. One day, she added a chopped-up chocolate bar to the **dough**. Ruth **published** her new **recipe** in 1938. A star cookie was born!

During **World War II**, families often mailed treats to soldiers overseas. Chocolate chip cookies quickly became known outside of Massachusetts!

Chocolate Chip Cookies Timeline

1930s
Ruth Wakefield invents the chocolate chip cookie

1939
Nestlé starts printing the chocolate chip cookie recipe on bags of chocolate chips

1950s
Refrigerated chocolate chip cookie dough is sold in stores

After the war, grocery stores sold refrigerated cookie dough and packaged cookies. Chocolate chip cookies became popular across the country.

Chocolate Chip Cookies Today

ice cream sandwiches

cookie dough

Today, stores sell cookie dough ice cream, cookie cakes, and cookie dough in a cup. People even enjoy sandwiches of ice cream between chocolate chip cookies!

Chocolate Chip Cookie Cake

Ask an adult to help you with this twist on the classic cookie.

Ingredients

- 3/4 cup butter
- 1 cup brown sugar
- 2 eggs
- 2 teaspoons vanilla extract
- 2 cups all-purpose flour
- 2 teaspoons cornstarch
- 1 teaspoon baking soda
- 1/2 teaspoon salt
- 1-1/2 cups chocolate chips

Instructions

1. Preheat oven to 350 degrees Fahrenheit (177 degrees Celsius). Grease cake pan.
2. Beat the butter until smooth. Add brown sugar and mix until creamy. Then mix in eggs and vanilla.
3. In the second bowl, stir flour, cornstarch, baking soda, and salt.
4. Slowly add the dry ingredients to the wet ingredients until combined. Add chocolate chips and stir.
5. Press the mixture evenly into the cake pan. Bake 15 minutes.
6. Cover cake with foil. Bake 5-10 more minutes, until cake is golden brown.
7. Remove from oven and let cool.
8. Decorate with frosting, M&Ms, or whatever you like!

Cookies come in many different **textures**. Some are soft and puffy. Others are crispy and crunchy. Some people love cookies that are burned on the bottom!

Make Your Perfect Cookie

Change to Ingredients	Cookie Texture
Add extra flour	➔ Puffier and crumblier
Chill dough for 24 hours	➔ Thicker and chewier
Melt butter	➔ Flatter with crispier edges
Use only brown sugar	➔ Softer with more butterscotch flavor

You can change the texture of your cookies by changing the way you bake them!

Different ingredients make different flavors. Some people add M&Ms or nuts to their cookies. Others add flavors like peanut butter or even strawberry!

Many people enjoy **vegan** cookies made without eggs or butter.

green tea chocolate chip cookies

strawberry white chocolate chip cookies

World's Largest Cookie

football field

size of world's largest cookie

100 yards (91.4 meters)

In 2003, a North Carolina bakery made the largest cookie ever. It was 101 feet (31 meters) across. It used 30,000 eggs and millions of chocolate chips.

Chocolate chip cookies are favorite snacks at any size!

Glossary

butterscotch—a flavor made from melted butter, brown sugar, and water

delicious—very tasty

dough—a thick mixture of mostly flour and liquid

ingredient—an item that helps make up a food

published—printed for a public audience

recipe—a set of instructions for making a specific food

textures—the way things feel when you touch them

vegan—made without any animal products

World War II—the war fought from 1939 through 1945 that involved many countries

To Learn More

AT THE LIBRARY
Ford, Gilbert. *How the Cookie Crumbled: The True (and Not-So-True) Stories of the Invention of the Chocolate Chip Cookie.* New York, N.Y.: Atheneum Books for Young Readers, 2017.

Kuskowski, Alex. *Super Simple Specialty Recipes: Easy Cookie Recipes for Kids!* Minneapolis, Minn.: Super Sandcastle, 2016.

Mathews, Charity. *Super Simple Baking for Kids.* Emeryville, Calif.: Rockridge Press, 2019.

ON THE WEB

FACTSURFER

Factsurfer.com gives you a safe, fun way to find more information.

1. Go to www.factsurfer.com.

2. Enter "chocolate chip cookies" into the search box and click 🔍.

3. Select your book cover to see a list of related web sites.

Index

baking, 4, 7, 8, 17
dessert, 5, 9
dough, 11, 13, 14
flavors, 18
history, 8, 9, 11, 12, 13, 20
how to make, 6
ice cream sandwiches, 14
ingredient, 6, 7, 18
Massachusetts, 9, 12
milk, 5
North Carolina, 20
published, 11
recipe, 10, 11, 15
snack, 4, 5, 21
soldiers, 12
stores, 13, 14
textures, 16, 17
timeline, 12
Toll House Inn, 8, 9
vegan, 18

Wakefield, Ruth, 8, 11
World War II, 12, 13
world's largest, 20

The images in this book are reproduced through the courtesy of: gowithstock, front cover; etorres, p. 3; Mandi J. Donohue, pp. 4-5; Carol Mellema, p. 5; Robyn Mackenzie, p. 6 (Step 1); SewCream, p. 6 (Step 2); SamaraHeisz5, p. 6 (Step 3), 6-7; Foodio, p. 6 (Step 4); Chronicle/ Alamy, pp. 8-9; Wikimedia Commons, p. 8 (bubble); Melica, p. 9; Martin Gardeazabal, p. 10; digital reflections, p. 11; Christina Leaf/ Bellwether Media, pp. 12-13; Elena Veselova, p. 14; Fascinadora, p. 14 (bubble); ODINTHEDOG/ Bellwether Media, p. 15; Astashov Yevhenii, pp. 16-17; everydayplus, p. 16; Naviya, p. 18; Mark McElroy, pp. 18-19; tlindsayg, pp. 21, 22.